Fairness

Kimberley Jane Pryor

MACMILLAN
LIBRARY

First published in 2010 by
MACMILLAN EDUCATION AUSTRALIA PTY LTD
15–19 Claremont Street, South Yarra 3141

Visit our website at www.macmillan.com.au or go directly
to www.macmillanlibrary.com.au

Associated companies and representatives throughout the world.

National Library of Australia Cataloguing-in-Publication entry

Pryor, Kimberley Jane, 1962–
    Fairness / Kimberley Jane Pryor.
    ISBN: 9781420278224 (hbk.)
    Pryor, Kimberley Jane, 1962– Values.
    Includes index.
    For primary school age.
    Fairness—Juvenile literature.
179.9

Managing Editor: Vanessa Lanaway
Editor: Helena Newton
Proofreader: Kirstie Innes-Will
Designer: Kerri Wilson
Page layout: Pier Vido
Photo researcher: Sarah Johnson (management: Debbie Gallagher)
Production Controller: Vanessa Johnson

Printed in China

Acknowledgements
The author and the publisher are grateful to the following for permission to reproduce copyright material:

Front cover photograph: Brother and sister playing board game at home, Monkey Business Images/Shutterstock

Photos courtesy of:
Jenny Acheson/Getty Images, **6**; Dorgie Productions/Getty Images, **22**; Monashee Frantz/Getty Images, **20**; Image Source/Getty Images, **10**; Jupiter Images/Getty Images, **13**; Jupiter Images/Getty Images, **15**; Jupiter Images/Getty Images, **28**; Richard Lewisohn/Getty Images, **19**; Dick Luria/Getty Images, **23**; Peter Mason/Getty Images, **5**; David Sacks/Getty Images, **18**; Baerbel Schmidt/Getty Images, **9**; Simon Watson/Getty Images, **26**; © Carmen Martinez Banús/iStockphoto, **12**; Jupiter Unlimited, **3**, **8**, **11**, **16**, **21**, **25**, **30**; Photolibrary, **14**; Alfred Abad/Photolibrary, **7**; Santa Clara/Photolibrary, **29**; Ragnar Schmuck/Photolibrary, **24**; Hill Street Studios/Photolibrary, **4**; Thomas Lauterbach/Photolibrary, **27**; © Monkey Business Images/Shutterstock, **1**, **17**.

While every care has been taken to trace and acknowledge copyright, the publisher tenders their apologies for any accidental infringement where copyright has proved untraceable. Where the attempt has been unsuccessful, the publisher welcomes information that would redress the situation.

For Nick, Ashley and Thomas

Contents

When a word is printed in **bold**, you can look up its meaning in the Glossary on page 31.

Values

Values are the things you believe in. They guide the way:

- you think
- you speak
- you **behave**.

Values help you to behave safely at a train station.

Values help you to decide what is right and what is wrong. They also help you to live your life in a meaningful way.

Values help you to follow the rules when racing toy boats.

Fairness

Fairness is treating all people in the right way.
It is making sure that some people are not treated
better or worse than others.

Giving everyone a turn
to hit a piñata is fair.

Fairness is also acting with **honesty**. It is doing activities and playing games by the rules.

Table tennis is more fun when every player plays by the rules.

Fair people

Fair people think carefully before making decisions. They think about how their decisions will affect others. They do not make decisions based only on what they will get.

Fair people only borrow one or two popular library books at a time, leaving some for others.

Fair people do not like to see others being treated unfairly. They stand up for their family, friends and neighbours.

People who do not wait their turn in line are treating others unfairly.

Being fair to family

Fair people do their best to share with other family members. They share toys, books and special treats.

It is fair to make sure each family member gets an ice-cream.

Fair people do not mind if other family members are given time and attention. They know that each family member deserves to feel special.

Fair people do not get jealous when other family members get attention on their birthdays.

Being fair to friends

Friends show fairness by listening to each other. They know that it is fair to talk sometimes and listen sometimes.

Good friends listen to each other.

Friends also show fairness by taking turns on play equipment. They have more fun when everyone gets a turn.

It is fair to wait for your turn to climb down a climbing net.

Being fair to neighbours

Fair people keep their pets in their own yards. They know that some neighbours may not like pets. They also know that some neighbours may be afraid of pets.

Good neighbours make sure that their dogs cannot escape from their yards.

Fair people also keep their belongings and their rubbish in their own yards. They do not allow these things to become litter in their neighbourhood.

You can help keep your neighbourhood clean by putting food scraps in a compost bin.

Ways to be fair

There are many different ways to be fair to your family, friends and neighbours. Treating all people **equally** is a good way to start being fair.

Fair people include both boys and girls in their games.

Taking turns and playing by the rules are also ways to be fair. Being **open-minded** is another way to practise fairness.

Taking turns to use your favourite coloured pencil is fair.

Treating all people equally

Treating all people **equally** is one way to be fair.
Fair people treat others with **kindness** and **respect**.

It is fair to treat everyone in your ballet class equally.

Fair people make friends with people from other **cultures**. They do not mind if their friends wear different clothing or have different **beliefs**.

People from different cultures can do homework together.

Taking turns

Taking turns is another way to be fair.
Fair people take turns using toys and play equipment.
They also take turns choosing music and movies.

Friends take turns choosing songs to listen to.

Fair friends take turns ringing each other up. They also take turns inviting each other to their homes or to other places.

Fair people remember when it is their turn to call their friends.

Playing by the rules

Playing by the rules is a part of fairness. Fair people make sure they understand the rules before they start playing a game.

Playing by the rules makes pool games fun for everyone.

In every game, one person will lose. Fair people play by the rules even when they are losing. They do not **cheat**, or **accuse** other people of cheating.

Fair draughts players always play by the rules.

Being open-minded

Being **open-minded** is a way to be fair to others. Open-minded people are able to accept new and different ideas.

It is fair to listen to a family member's ideas about good food.

Open-minded people also listen to all sides of a story. Then they decide what they will believe.

Listening to someone else's side of a story is one way to be open-minded.

Admitting to making mistakes

Fair people admit to making mistakes. They fix their mistakes as soon as they can. They do their best to make up for what they have done wrong.

If you hurt a friend's feelings, it is a good idea to apologise.

When fair people make mistakes, they try to find out why. They do not blame others unfairly, or blame their equipment.

Blaming your skates when you fall over is not admitting to your mistakes.

Not taking advantage of others

Fair people do not take advantage of others. When they play games with others, they take turns to do different jobs. They also share out jobs around the home evenly.

It is unfair if one person does all the work while another plays.

Fair people do not do the wrong thing when others are not watching. They do not spend more time playing computer games than they are allowed to.

Playing computer games all day when other family members need help is unfair.

Personal set of values

There are many different values. Everyone has a personal set of values. This set of values guides people in big and little ways in their daily lives.

An umpire must make fair decisions at a baseball game.

Glossary

accuse	blame someone for doing something wrong
behave	act in a certain way
beliefs	things that people believe and accept as true
cheat	break the rules in a sneaky way
cultures	skills, arts, beliefs, customs and language that groups of people share
equally	the same
honesty	truthfulness and fairness
kindness	being friendly and noticing when others need help
open-minded	able to accept new and different ideas
respect	treating others the way you would like to be treated

Index